# IN THE GARDEN OF HAPPINESS

*dodinsky*

Illustrations by Ignacio G.

sourcebooks

Published by Sourcebooks, Inc.
P.O. Box 4410, Naperville, Illinois 60567-4410
(630) 961-3900
Fax: (630) 961-2168
www.sourcebooks.com

Printed and bound in China.
LEO 10 9 8 7 6 5 4 3 2 1

Dear Readers,
When life is tough and seems overwhelming,
it is my ardent hope that the simple reminders in this book
will help center your thoughts and lift up your spirit.

*always remember:*
"The magnitude of your life is proportional
to the magnitude of your thoughts."

*—dodinsky*

No matter how much negativity is thrown at **YOU**
by others, there is no need for you to stay and partake
in the decay they have chosen for their own lives.

YOU decide how your soul grows.

Happy people don't go through life
collecting and seeking recognition.

They go through life
*giving it away.*

Sometimes life's DISTRACTIONS will lead you away from the real journey. Broken DREAMS, broken *relationships...* and you mistakenly think that you are broken too.

If you've strayed too far, it only takes a few steps **to bring yourself back home.**

You will find that you are still
as *complete* as the day you were born.
Never broken, just distracted.

The heart has room for many opinions,
but you don't need to entertain all of them.

Some thoughts can be harmful to your happiness
if you hold on to them for too long.

To live fully, you must practice kindness.
You have to *breathe it in* and then *breathe it out*.

You get
*angry.*

You get
*stressed.*

You
*worry.*

But never let these feelings
consume your life.
You owe it to yourself
not to burden your soul
with sorrows.

You have to leave
the past behind and
STRIVE TOWARD
HAPPINESS.

There are times when you must cross a bridge, and there are times when you must burn it.

But keep building ONE and **never lose faith in life.**

If you are unsure of your purpose,
fill your days with moments
that bring joy to your life, even
the silliest or smallest of things.

When you feed your *heart*
with things that *delight* you,
they will illuminate your path
to **HAPPINESS.**

Everyone you meet brings *illumination* to your life—even those who have caused you pain.

That message is harder to find when you are hurting,
but once you discover the lesson behind the pain,
it might just be the most brilliant light you need to
*brighten* the rest of your *journey*.

If you are in despair, BELIEVE that there is always a better place, a better time, and a better person for you. Always have faith that something BETTER awaits you.

Steer your thoughts away from
being trapped in the past so you can
accomplish new and better things
in the present.

Sometimes you do not see
your own *strength* because it
is hidden from you by two people:
yourself and the person who
benefits from your weakness.

Cruelty—if you allow it—can subdue your spirit. You must not let darkness descend upon your heart by letting the actions of others cloud your sunshine.

We think we are like a little branch that quivers during a storm, doubting our strength, but we forget that we are the tree—deeply rooted to *withstand* all of life's upheavals.

When you decide to graduate from your regrets and disappointments, there is a brilliant career waiting for you called **LIFE.**

Whenever you manage to *smile*
in spite of the hardships you're facing,
it means your soul is refusing to be a
prisoner of your own sorrows.

A *peaceful man* is not free from
the pinch of life's aggravations.
He simply DECLINES to give them power
and refuses to be held captive by them.

No one can pull
you down if you raise
your awareness
of your own inner
*strength* and *beauty*.

You can find inspiration from others,
but **DETERMINATION** is solely your responsibility.

Don't travel too far away from
the **child within you**, and never
abandon the sense of *wonder* that
can magnify the smallest of things
into a mountain of *joy*.

When you lose sight of happiness, the child
within can guide you back to the things
that will NOURISH YOUR HEART.

Some people cannot stand that you are
moving on with your life. They will try to
hinder your progress by digging up the past.

Do not help them by acknowledging their behavior.
Keep moving forward and leave them behind with your past.

Stop seeking acceptance from people who
relentlessly ignore you. Every inch of progress
you make toward their approval will be a mile
farther away from your self-worth.

To find the star that sparkles the most,
you need to look inward—because
not all stars are settled in the sky.

May you gather the strength to HOLD ON to your dreams and *follow your passion* when others are trying to diminish your worth.

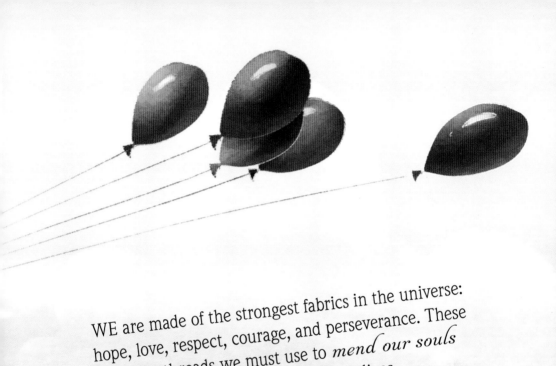

WE are made of the strongest fabrics in the universe: hope, love, respect, courage, and perseverance. These are the threads we must use to *mend our souls* when misfortune tears our lives.

Do not carry the broken parts of your aspirations
with you if they only serve to injure your spirit.

Find the courage to release the
mournful attachments you have with
the past, and start tending to the seeds
of new beginnings in your heart.

To shed a tear is not always
a sad thing. Sometimes a teardrop is a
*wonderful* thought or a joyful memory
leaving your heart to *frolic* on your cheek.

It is sometimes the uphill struggles that will give you the best view of life's most forgotten and beautiful landscapes.

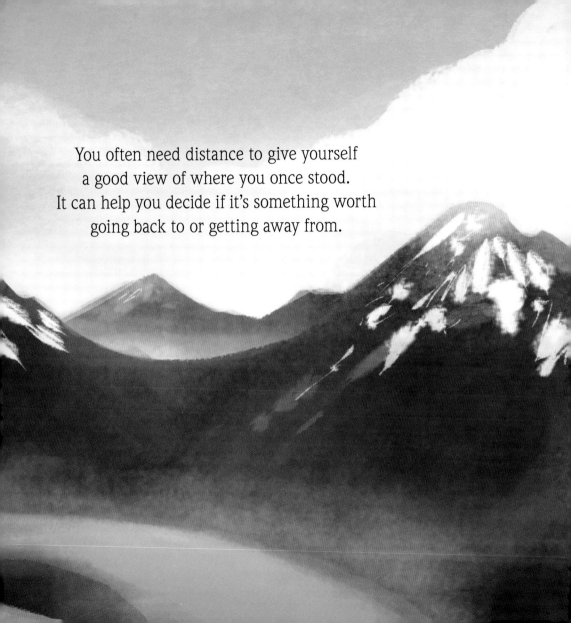

You often need distance to give yourself
a good view of where you once stood.
It can help you decide if it's something worth
going back to or getting away from.

When someone leaves you,
it DOESN'T give you permission
to run away from yourself too.

NEVER deny or
waste an opportunity
*to be kind to others*,
even if some people have
been unkind to you.
The two are not related.

Disengage your life from anger,
sadness, and insecurity.
You must detach yourself from people
who repeatedly contribute
to those feelings.

It is not your responsibility to help people who willfully build their own prisons. You have to identify who needs help and who simply craves attention.

As we search for our truth, we
cross paths with those seeking their own.

We discover that life's many roads lead to a shared destination,
and that our days are valued not by worldly possessions, but by
the amount of *treasures* the heart has gathered.

There are times when you need to explain your actions
to others out of respect. But accept the fact that some people
don't really care about what you say or do.

There are times when you need to stop explaining
out of *respect* for YOURSELF.

Do not reciprocate the acts of malice and hurt
others have brought into your life. You might get
used to being VENGEFUL, and become good at it.

There's so much more you can do with your life.
Reducing yourself to who they are is not one of them.

When something bad happens,
the momentary disruption in your life seems irreparable
when you are looking at it with a defeated attitude.

Life's troubles are meant to **toughen** you,
THEN PASS THROUGH.

They will not stay
permanently without your
personal invitation.

When you're feeling tired of being miserable
and it's breaking you down, don't ever fold.
You owe it to yourself to TRY to become
*the best person you can be.*
There are days when all you can do is just TRY.

All the unfair things people bring into your life
must not lead you astray from finding the
*best things you can give to yourself.*

If you allow momentary defeats to find shelter in your heart, you are allowing your most BEAUTIFUL DREAMS to become homeless.

Do not allow yourself to get angry
over what others think about you.
Some people belittle others
to make themselves feel better.

They seem to believe that STEPPING
on others will elevate their stature in life.

We have to remind ourselves that when people bear down on us, sometimes stepping away, instead of pushing back, will better serve our *inner peace*.

You forgive because you want to build a stronger **relationship with yourself** and NOT with the ones who hurt you.

Some people will never "get you."
Do not spend an eternity asking why,
because everyone will see you differently.
It is paramount to your happiness to
**cherish those who** *lift your soul*.

**HAPPINESS IS**

when your heart gives little attention
to opinions that demean your *spirit*.

The STRONGEST people are those who can restrain themselves
from throwing hurtful words. Even if they know they can,
it does not mean they should.

Anger has a way of inflicting injury on another,
but leaves you wounded too.

When things fall apart, do not scold your heart
by filling it with insecurities. Rise up and say to
yourself, "Not today, not a chance, and not ever.
**LIFE is calling me!"**

You GROW where you are appreciated.
You wither where you are taken for granted.
Choose WHERE you want your *soul to dwell*.

If you fixate on people's opinions, it leaves you vulnerable to self-doubt and insecurity. If left unchecked, their opinions will invade your life and wound your spirit.

## HAPPINESS IS

discovering that the most worthwhile
validation is the one you give to yourself.

No matter what you have gone through
and what others have put you through,
*you are still you.*

Embrace happiness.
Find your passion.
Love yourself.
These things can never be
taken away from you.
Nothing can stop you
from rediscovering yourself.

The greatest journey always begins within YOU.

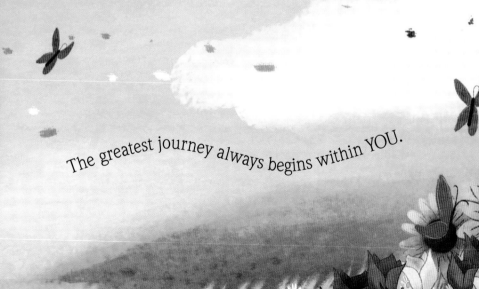

## IT TAKES A VILLAGE TO CREATE A BOOK:

A huge THANK YOU goes to my editor Dana, for perfecting the thoughts in this book, and to my illustrator Ignacio, whose artworks breathe life into them.

My deep appreciation to the miraculous art department of Sourcebooks—Helen, Kelly, and especially Brittany—for helping me achieve my vision for this book.

To the "village folks" in my life (Arthur Galindo, Carolyn, Wendy, and Shana), know that I am truly blessed and inspired by the amount of faith you have in me.